I0682891

Redemptive Musings

Redemptive Musings

Editor
Bina Singh
Convener

Editorial Board
Niharika Lal, Organizing Secretary
Annapurna
Bharati Chattopadhyay

Patron
Rachna Srivastava
Principal

HAWAKAL

HAWAKAL

Published by Hawakal Publishers
185 Kali Temple Road, Nimta, Kolkata 700049
India

in collaboration with

Vasant Kanya Mahavidyalaya
Kamachha, Varanasi
Accredited 'A' by NAAC
(Admitted to the privileges of Banaras Hindu University)

Email info@hawakal.com
Website www.hawakal.com

First edition September, 2019

Copyright © Individual Poets 2019
All rights reserved

Cover design: Bitan Chakraborty

ISBN: 978-93-87883-84-0
Price: 400 INR | USD 13.99

Editor's Note

The world is heading towards an alarming state of anarchy and chaos. Human civilization is on the verge of extinction as humanity is turning into a barbaric reality. The demonic forces of terrorism, promoting hatred and violence is disrupting the peace and harmony of existence. Consequently, living in an emotionally, morally and spiritually sterile world, the greatest challenge before mankind is how to save the fractured humanity. The graph of degeneration continues to increase with shadowed pseudo wisdom and pseudo religious cultural faith. Thus, the perplexed mortals, helplessly beat their wings in the ghastly void.

Since time immemorial saints and seers with their profound wisdom have advocated and enlightened humanity in realising the positive values that have perpetually healed,soothed and sustained existence. In this regard literary thinkers too with their poignantly powerful literary reflections have stood for humanity. Literature and life, the two sides of the same coin have ceaselessly portrayed life in totality, upholding values that enrich and empower the bliss of living. In this respect poetry being one of the oldest literary genres, with it's cathartic power has incessantly contributed towards the upliftment of humanity. In this context Wordsworth's claim that poet is a man speaking to men , providing a healing touch to the afflicted humanity, needs to be reconsidered. Poet the seeker of the absolute truth, through his lyrical cravings can be the desired shield to fight the evil powers in order to restore love peace and harmony in each and all. Thus Arnold"s assertion that poetry is a voice from the inmost soul, a thing of Beauty and Joy forever, making life richer and fuller is essentially still relevant in awakening the dormant mortals from their slumber.

Kashi, the city of lights, has a glorious and peerless heritage of immortal poets like Kabir, Ravidas and Tulsidas, who have relentlessly, through their creative compositions, rendered songs of faith, supporting love, peace and harmony. In this regard, I quote Kabir: "पोथी पढ़ पढ़ जग मुआ पंडित भया न कोय ढाई आखर प्रेम का पढ़े सो पंडित होय". These immortal words continue to inspire and enlighten humanity even today. Abiding with the lofty poetic tradition of Kashi, Department of English, Vasant Kanya Mahavidyalaya, has organized an International Poetry Festival. In this great meet of poets from India and abroad, a book of poems-*Redemptive Musings* has been published, celebrating the power of the Muse.

Dr. Bina Singh
Convener
International Poetry Festival
Vasant Kanya Mahavidyalaya, Varanasi

Preface

"Poetry is simply the most beautiful, impressive and widely effective mode of saying things, and hence its importance." – Matthew Arnold.

Undeniably, poetry is the sublimest of all literary forms, yet it defies a concrete definition. According to some, it is the language of emotions and passions, to others it is related to imagination and still others hold it to be an art infused with intonation, rhythm and music. Moreover, there are still other people who hold it to be a blessing, bestowed upon a privileged few and it is these people who have the potential to create a good poem. But despite the exalted place provided to it, the journey of poetry has not been a smooth one. It has had to face severe criticism in the hands of Plato, Macaulay and others but at the same time it was fortunate enough to have staunch adherents like Aristotle, Sidney, Shelley to name a few who have presented strong cases in its favour. Moreover, it has had to face a strong competition in the form of the novel but its surging popularity today proves what W.Somerset Maugham had said – "the crown of literature is poetry".

In all ages, nations and cultures, poets have been placed on a very high pedestal. A poet is perceived to be a creator and visionary who can envision the past, present and future and enter into those realms of existence and consciousness where even the sunbeams cannot penetrate - जहाँ न जाये रवि, तहाँ जाये कवि. He not only gives voice to his feelings and perceptions but also addresses the problems and needs of the age. As pointed out by Dylan Thomas, "A good poem is a contribution to reality. The world is never the same once a good poem has been added to it. A good poem helps to change the shape of the universe, helps to extend everyone's knowledge of himself and the world around him. It also helps in liberating the poet from the constraints of time and space.

The poet has a two-fold task while composing a poem – (1) to express himself and (2) to give his expression a proper structure. A good poem must essentially have both form and content. A poet draws on his experiences and impressions and it are these that form the raw material of poetry. When he puts them in a proper order through the selection of words, then that becomes the form or structure. The first stage is a mental process and the second is its outer projection. The second stage requires the power of composition, of organizing memories, associations and impressions into an organic form. The poet strives to transmit the emotion to the reader in precisely the same manner as he had experienced it. The language becomes sublime and symbolic and even if the idioms and phrases are of everyday life, they take on a different connotation. If a poem loses its sublimity, it fails to appeal to the reader and this is what a poet should be wary of. Poets take a lot of liberty with form and language but it should be kept in mind that rhythm, beat and music are essential elements of poetry. If they are found lacking, then it loses its charm. On the other hand, when the focus is only on the rhyming scheme, metre and structure without any emotional content, then, too, poetry loses its aesthetic value. Thus, a poet has to make a conscious effort to strike a balance between form and content, using words, imagery and rhythm in such a way that they do not detract from the impression he is trying to convey.

Today, we are living in a world that is wrought by conflicts, chaos and disorder. The lofty ideals and values of our ancestors are crumbling down depriving man of his humanist sensibilities. It is in times like this that poetry can become an important medium to restore peace and harmony as it appeals to and expresses man's sensitivity. Moreover, it stimulates him and provides him with the courage and strength to overcome the adversities of life. As has been aptly said by Mahmoud Darwish, a Palestinian poet, "Poetry and Beauty are always making peace. When you read something beautiful you find coexistence; it breaks walls down."

It is a momentous occasion for us that poets not only from India but abroad have contributed to the present anthology, making it rich and varied. It is hoped that it will be received with appreciation in the literary world and will encourage aspiring poets in their endeavours.

Dr. Niharika Lal
Organizing Secretary
International Poetry Festival
Vasant Kanya Mahavidyalaya, Varanasi

May I wish all success to this adventure--an international poetry festival organized by this fine college which still flags the memory of Annie Besant. May the festival bring out some scorching poetry.

Keki N. Daruwalla

CONTENTS

ANEETA CHITALE

Elixir

Clad in transparent, drenched, wet in
Waters' splash
On my wet skin, lits' up in fire
It's better than my naked brown skin getting
Bare, brazen!

The layers, so silken, draped around me reflects
Like pearls in ocean,from ocean surfs-
On the sea shores, rising waves!

I always love the first touch of fluorescent water,
Crystalline water sprung from celestial waves…
It waxes my skin, sparkling my body
With exotic dreams!

Absolves my carnal pangs, of love
Some blemished, some char'd
Some impressed with love bites
All changing
With the seasons, of life
Evanescence!
All smoothens out lovingly in
Crystalline waters, caressed
On my wet skin!

A little thin veil, transparent cover
On my wet skin, kindles the fire within
In a splash!

I have died a thousand deaths
Yet reborn again
Time's vain dance!

In splash of water!
Healing my wounds, rejuvenating
My body and weary soul!
To sparkle again… with the chime of
Pious "Temple Bells"
Crystalline water…
Elixir of Life!

ANTONIO J RIVAS MELEAN

Beloved

The longing to fly to the mountains
Navigating between words of verses
The timelessness of the soulmates..

Holy grail looking for happiness
Meeting with our beloved love
Among the mirages
Of the remoteness ...

The wildness among dark shadows
The scattering shadows with sunlight
Looking for brightness
In our hearts...

Only she is my beloved
She grows with our desire
When we go in deep inside her...

In slow flow in its deep center
The longed storm of the storms
We die and we are reborn in bliss...

Again and again until dawn
The spell of the twin souls
The memories of past lives...

Loving our secret silences

The conspiracy of the lovers
Illuminating our own heavens
The torment of my torments...

GEORGE ONSY

Divino – Human Ecstacy 1

Some say Eros... others wine
To satiate that eternal thirst
Yet, getting lost in your
Cosmic hug,
My-very-self is no more mine.

ISAH WISDOM

Internal Smile

Symmetric mountain carries the sublime symphony
of enlivened sound,
the subtle waterfalls cascade the meaning of life to the
boisterous winds,
the graceful fountain builds a resonate bridge of attraction,
the spring of musical actors gush spontaneously to the theatre
of serene rock,
the meadows advertise the productive services of the prudent
brook,
as the spectator trees raise their placard to caress the anointed
kisses of the falls,
The rain becomes the prevalent Empress during her reign,
but inside her droplets a reel of tears still shapes,
this holler of drops doesn't seal her seal,
she chooses to ripple her blessing unto Nature's Kingdom,
The ecstacy of the Sun does her altruistic work on the face of
the ample cerulean,
She sells liberally wonderful shine to her receptive patron,
within the ephemeral speeches of time,
the exuberant sky exchanges pleasantries of goodness with the
carefree Sun,
she knows what lies gloom inside her skin,
and when the moment comes,

she ventures into the fabrics of the nocturnal dark,
despite the dim state she still grins life to the night linen ,
When the rage of heavy storm screams loudly on the earth,
the aerial bird doesn't wish to sink into the ocean deep,
for after the blustery tumult ,
she shall once again unfurl her wings,
and sing with mellifluous melody the music in her heart,
When tempest of undulating turbulence arises,
the creatures of the sea,
never wish to migrate from their houses to live on the land of the roses,
she imbibes an internal smile.

JYOTIRMAYA THAKUR

Cadences

Every moment is a requiem of delight,
Every memory an euphony of light.

Just start through the startling haze,
With the child's eyes of innocent gaze.

Play your part with amazing grace,
Pains and joys are chapters of the race.

Music resounds with the lovers voice,
Songs with fragrance of frankincense.

Doors of a room open like book of spells,
Charged with magic from deepest wells.

Dreams float on beautiful cadences ,
As they drift through the severe woods .

Layers of boredom,layers of guilt,
Lifting weight of a million worlds built.

MARY LYNN LUIZ

My Perfect Rose

Your blooming, slowly opening like the petals of a rose
I'm blessed to watch as the bud begins to unfold!
So many mysteries I see in your beautiful bright eyes,
How long will they lay hidden, before to me, you expose?
Your face glows giving radiance to this place,
with an aura that sheds so much love and grace!
Your beauty is unimaginable and overwhelming,
to my heart, is so drawing, absolutely compelling!
I'm a slave to all of your wonderful and magical ways,
And I will be excited to experience them all of my days!
Captivated by all of your whims and charms,
as our love is kept safe and warm, in each other's arms!
For my heart's garden, so long ago, you consented to be mine!
With passing of time, tender loving care, and the help of The
Divine
Your hand in mine, My Beloved, in my heart, you're forever
enshrined
You've grown from a bud, to become, My Perfect Rose!

MUHAMMAD SHANAZAR

My Dreams Will Dangle Down

Life is in the jaws of death
And I dream for my descendants
The earth as a peaceful planet
I stand forlorn in the wilderness
And look with curiosity to all directions,
For commodities that may nourish my generation,
But I sniff the smell of exploded explosives,
It has dulled my all senses,
Now I don't yearn for
The fragrance of jasmine or roses,
Nor I yearn for the touch of unravished petals,
As now I have formed my opinion,
The warriors are resolute
To make the planet sterile,
On some day all bombs and shells will explode,
Smoke will engulf the earth from all sides,
And my dreams will dangle down,

On the tassels of impossibilities.

SHAHID ABBAS

Rage Takes Many Forms

The news has been so sad lately
It seems as if the earth is on fire
Rage takes many forms
Eruptions and tsunamis are not uncommon
After all aren't we humans quick to anger
That tidal wave of tears are those shed by widows and orphans
the left behinds and the consequence of bad decisions
Made by bad men
We need to change our thinking
The Brotherhood of Mankind needs fixing
We need to share more
Fight less
And always choose kindness above all else
Be peaceful
We were fashioned that way...

TARIQ MUHAMMAD

Soul of a Flower

Walking one day in the backwoods
Melancholy and gloom
On a low hanging bough I saw
A radiant flower in full bloom.

The gentle breeze fluttered it's folds
The flower returned a smiling stance
Dumbfounded I realized that
Witnessed I had an incredible chance.

The flower seemed to beckon me
Drawing me by its lustrous hue
Flora and fauna many I've seen
But this one bore a bizarre clue.

It seemed to say "let me be"
Enticing and beautiful on the tree
Pluck me and you'll break my heart
I'll wither and die without a spree.

Smiling to myself I left the flower
In its own gorgeous reincarnation
Maybe it was the soul of
A wretch or some great manifestation

MAJA HERMAN SEKULIĆ

The Lady of Vincha

Canto I
I saw her who was I
How bent as willow
Hums while polishing clay floor
To its highest glow
While admiring herself, vain,
As in mirror

Then you ran through the fields free
With breeze of the blessed day
Sculpted birds with wings spread
After noon, after work, relaxed
You walked upright bareheaded, blond,
Golden, fairy like

I saw how with hawthorn twigs
You start kilns you built
Their burnt wickers - your stylus and scepter
Beyond good and evil is your power –
You spread your might benevolent
Over us, over mankind
From the beginning of time

Without knowing it

I watched you transverse, light-footed,
Full length of a meadow, well built,
How you glide among willows, pregnant,
Along the lazy Danube banks, braiding yellow locks
How you ride wild bulls, beautiful,
To the mines of Avala mount

I saw how you plant seeds, lentils and wheat,
And clear whole forests, thick virginal woods,
Like a fire, unstoppable, quick,
How you lay in the deep magic grass
How you catch fireflies in bowl for secret rituals
Protecting willow trees from any harm all the while

Because you bend when needed, like a twig,
You throw yourself thoughtless in man's arms
Feminine, bejeweled, and yet stone like, unbreakable,
White like leprosy with black mask
Our mother, the sacred Mistress of our lives
And death, our prophet,
And our witch - sinless

You invoke your white-faced Muses, sisters, priestesses,
To dance, to pray for miners in the orgiastic trance
When they come from Earth to lay tired in your embrace
Bringing you shells and crystals, malachite and cinnabar,
Over seven hills and seven seas, from the end of the world,
To renew their masculine strength in your lap

You invoke magic for those who draw
Signs who tell of holy trees you worship

Of dreams in you, in them, in me,
Of birds, of sacred snakes, monsters,
Of river shallows and maelstroms,
Of sheep and bulls on glossy bowls.

As if I read your mind
I saw you who were I
I saw how mighty and how innocent you are
Big-eyed goddess beyond good and bad
I saw the first book in the world
You have written in your head

Without knowing it

SELVAM V. PUJARI

Love became a fancy

I am not a royal by now, but then
My adventures of love are sacred
As Varuruchi, a defamed brahman
Gave a Sakhuntalai an adieu bond
Never keep bevy of queens by a chief
Grave causes of emotional pursuits
On pity thoughts resulted in to suffer
Offered couple of great humiliations
Folly of two of matchless by souls
To a beauty, and another's on time
Praise of my pitying heart and grace
Their instant sensation put in Harem
With tremendous woes and sufferings
I found, to fall in love on pure nymphs.

ANCHAL RANA

Death Says

I, a wanderer in this forsaken land.
Bestowed upon me this oath..
Peregrinating in perpetuity
Hauling the ashen taste of this counterfeit humanity.

The embers of the fiery fire
Once illuminating this darkened world.
Now is fazed and weakened.
Grimacing , I fare the vales of malignance.

Your fate intertwined but you are sheared in diverging faiths.
A receding catastrophe plundering you of your morality.
You worship gilded walls of terrorism.
Wistfully I hover to see penury ascending.

Hurling past the facade you wear
Embellished , radiating a scornful affair.
Humans fearing me whereas I contemplate
Am I worse than pestilence , war and genocide they themselves
initiate?

O' heavens I don a cloak of despair!
Yet the resentment here vanquished me in amazement.
You are plotting your own end, in the name of development.
You can't avert oblivion . For I am death.

PRIYA S. BHARDWAJ

Memories

When the crimson moon drenched
the night, with it came the old ties

Quivering memories trickled
from her eyes,

Creases of memory lane formed
On her contorted face,
Vanished in pain the sparkle of her eyes,
I heard my name in her dejected cries.

The desire to taste the pearl on her lips,
To feel the breathing breeze in her locks ,
 Trying to Grasp the inconceivable shadows ,
Lifted my hands towards the limitless ,
Searching you in the formless clouds .

Sitting by the side of vault,
Carrying a cold frame of heart ,
From evening to eternal night ,
Revolves the spectacle of past ,
Embracing it all, in peace I slept.

PRAMILA KHADUN

Amazon is burning

Amazon is burning and with it, my heart is burning.
The fire was not created by slamming of two stones,
Nor did lightning fall from the sky
To create this mayhem of ravage.

Can Planet earth without the Amazon be envisioned?
The nuclear super powers committed
To global security and safety of environment
Must save Amazon, the lungs of the globe.
We are living in an era of herd mentality
Where people care more for themselves
And lesser for what is around them.

Deforestation is affecting our oxygen supply,
Injuring our health and the pristine beauty of nature.
Our rainfall is threatened and with it our crops.
Thinkers of exceptional sensitivity,
Responsible botanists and men and women
Poised and savvy, shocked to the core
Are waiting for a panacea for this evil.
Like moth to flame, we are drawn
To the illusion of materialism
At the cost of putting Mother Nature on her knees.

Amazon, like the phoenix, rise from your ashes.
The orangutans are beating their chests,

The rabbits stunned and the colorful birds
Are fluttering their wings in agony.
So many species of animals and plants are affected.

May nations across the globe unite their efforts
To stop this burning and smoldering
Of our beautiful Amazon, so loving, so motherly.
Save Amazon!

SUDEEP SEN

Prayer Flag

Om Ma Ni Padme Hum
O the Jewel in the Lotus
   —Inscription on a Tibetan prayer flag

1. MANAS SAROVAR, MT. KAILASH

Frayed, flapping in the high winds —
 prayer flags gently unravel —
homage to the day's first light.

But today, the dawn is not as bright,
though heavy, brooding, silver-grey
like the lake's shimmering glass-top.

No one is here, except for a woman
  staring far away,
wrapped in her sanctity

of continuous linen — her own sari
like a prayer flag —
though devoid of any colour.

She isn't mourning or crying,
  just gazing fixedly
into the water's changing glimmer,

as the sky's wet weight
 and the shore's rocky line meet,
their edges meanderingly

melting into the lake itself.
 I stood far behind her,
behind everything she saw.

2. PRAYER FLAGS

She was only
  an accidental figure
in the wide-screen frame.

Unlike her,
  I was looking skywards,
through the prayer flag's

translucent cotton,
  counting each thread
of each piece of cloth

that wove private stories,
  whispered *only* to me.
Weather-worn, strung across

canted multiple horizons,
  I tried to map
their own geographies —

each an island,
  each with its own terrain, texture,
inscription, and scripture.

Found on the highest points
  on land, as close to the sky
as is possible,

these magic carpets —
  shapes caught on
an unintentional clothes-line —

were more meaningful to me
  than this vast
monastic scenery.

How each flag — each one,
  must have preserved secrets
that *only* their owners knew.

How each, a talisman —
  exuded safety and calm —
shrouding away grief

for the briefest while,
  when one forgets everything —
real, imagined — and just dreams.

3. **PILGRIMAGE**

My own piece of cloth
  that I'd once tied onto this line,
wasn't visible to me now.

But that did not matter.
  I found strength in this
procession of private passion,

in these flags' lack of starch
   or hierarchy.
Their stories passed down

by one flag to another,
   toggled hand in hand
through time and age —

just like my pet yellow butterfly
   who infused each flower
in my garden with the gift of life

without any show or fare. I like
   the transparent quiet here — I also
like the wind's occasional sound,

its severe current tearing through
   the flag's heart—picking out
the perfect pitch and melody.

4. BUDDHA IN A LOTUS

A memory now, a still — framed,
   not revealing to the world
what I had once seen —

the panorama's generosity,
   its wild, stark untouchability.
How each story

stitched and preserved
   like the jewel in the lotus —
its crystal-fine edges

caressed by petal's soft skin —
  until,
everything folds inward —

like a foetus in a womb,
  a toppled misplaced comma,
my own implanted memory.

And then, they bloom,
  fanning outward —
each flag, strand, story,

each private grief and pleasure —
  chanting noiselessly
in the mountain's silent winds.

JERNAIL SINGH ANAND

Man: The Super Power

The electric wires are so fragile yet the mission they carry is
monumental.
The life that runs through their flexible body
breaks through the mountains
And pierces the heart of darkness.

Do they ever resist when they are coiled
And pushed behind electricity boards?
Tag them here or hang them there
Never utter a sigh.

But, once connected to the source,
They turn live,
And lo! The fragile vesture now
Acquires the power delivered by dams
And runs warships and aeroplanes.

Man too is ductile metal,
Highly manipulable in body and mind,
And to look at,
Just another animal albeit a bit improved.

But the moment he connects himself to the
Source divine,
Now a super power makes
Oceans subside and even turns the tide.

ANIL DESHWAL DAS

A Boy and Sea

Far flung in an island,
there was a tree a boy and sea.

No ships no boats no men did ever went by thee.

The boy made a house
of leaves thatch and stick.

He went in search in Island
and found fire a pipe and weed.

And years rolled by,
he ate and slept and smoked the weed.

He never thought of anything,
and there was ever no such need.

Then came a girl floating
from a broken boat deep from the sea

Once when she was alright
he proposed and she married thee

A few more years as went by
they had a baby,
air was filled with fun love laughter and glee.

He made a bigger house
much far from his tree and sea.

Now daily he goes in search for food
and she accompanies he.

They look after the house
which is far from the sea.

He is now a man who is lost in his home and the time
And long forgotten
are the boy the tree the and the sea.

ANKITA PATHAK

Adiyogi

On the edge of the morning,
A ray decended, blinding my eyes,
been taken out of the world ,
where the grasses jeweled up as Emerald,
eyes felt the bluish feathery touch,
Mesmerised by his glamour.
Oh! The Divine.
Emerged as an outsketch figured by a sketcher
The Supreme Fire of Determination,
Anger, Passion and Love.
Redeemer of both the worlds: The Heaven and The Hell

Appearing the mighty Aniconic power of Lingam,
Wearing five serpents as ornaments.
Immersed fathomlessly in meditation,
Sparked! Posing as a cosmic dancer,
The smile underlined his figure.

Blessed and Courageous did I feel;
By the throbs of the masculine
Unperturbed ;agitating like the sea.
Fire his head, the sun and moon his eyes,
Vedas his speech, the winds his breath
By thine's damru beats –
Evil shakes! While the Wises awake!

Oh! The representator of the non-dualistic absolute,
Thine's seeds dwells in each hearts, down the centuries
From the sources of vibrant consciousness;
As Shiva is Shakti and Shakti is Shiva.

ARINDAM ROY

Himabindu: A Varanasi Love Song

Maria to me was Himabindu–
A Greek girl, danseuse, singer and beloved of many births.
A girl with blue eyes of Varanasi's dawn,
The blue of Shiva's throat.

Performing Shiva Tandava,that evening, she destroyed and
Created, a dark, sultry girl – a Jamini Roy painting –

An Indian princess, in her earlier avatar.
And then, she became Tagore's *Krishnakoli*...

Among jasmine and songs –
We were a tangle of arms and legs,
A tireless love poem of many a poet.

The crumpled white sheet of our hotel bed in Varanasi,
Mapped our desires, as
Ganga howled outside the window all night;
We were unmindful of the stench of charred flesh of corpses
Mingling with jasmine.

"Deaths are births too, my Love,"
"What will you call me then?" she asked.
"That answer, my Love,
Is in the womb of Time."

ARUNA SRI MEDIPALLY

Varanasi

Holy city Spiritual city
Divine city Cultural city
Serene city Unique city
Eternal City Historical city
City of temples Religious capital

Older than history
Older than tradition
Older even than legend
Benares Kashi Varanasi
Kashi is greater than Heaven

Holy dip in Sacred Ganges
Washes away all of our sins
Hindus want to die at Kashi
Get to be cremated here
To get salvation
Want to visit at least once
In their life time to get Moksha

Lord Kashi Vishwanatha and Mother Vishalakshi
Spreading happiness everywhere
City of light and enlightenment
Our Kashi Varanasi

BHAGIRATH CHOWDHARY

The Cosmic Leadership

Sacred Vow of Universal Welfare must form,
The core of the very organism's form,
Like water, no insistence on own ego identity,
Only Universal Welfare must embody the Divine Entity.

Like God Particle Field of Cosmic Will as Central Pillar of
Light,
The Divine Entity must give mass to make everyone truly
bright,
To end Cosmic Uncertainty and give sovereignty to all,
Creating infinite field of choices be as own attributes on call.

Egoless benevolent existence needs nothing to defend,
Divine Entity has evolutionary urge its only weapon to contend,
Time like hour glass becomes its musical instrument,
Sounding a Clarion Call to all to rise as entities so benevolent.

Conscious Mind atop as moon crescent so very benevolent,
Ready to receive divine attributes of Cosmic Mind so potent,
Let Will of Universal Welfare rise as holy river of living water,
Flow on awaiting earth to build a welfare ecosystem so better.

Being focused on the Central Pillar of Light as only Volition,
Allowing one and all a cosmic field of welfare for evolution,
Will of Universal Welfare embodied makes a Cosmic Leader,
I bow down to that Deity of Kashi -Vishwanath as my leader.

BINAY LAHA

Auction of my soul

Off is the wind
Off is the mind.
Go and pick up the missing spine
When you are drowsy in a sumptuous dine.
Off is the word.
Off is the poem.
Come and help to make me bird
Though we know to fly is hard.
Off is the world.
Off are the lives.
We will start after deathly revive.
We will write, we will write.

BRAJESH KUMAR GUPTA "MEWADEV"

View Of Burning Love

People can understand you
Of passing clouds and falling tears
The true condition of widows
Where burning love shuttered in pain
But when your casket closes
I know not where to turn
But with our hearts broken apart will it ever be the time
Behind woven webs,
Too frightened, too shocked, too ignorant
Then breath has gone raising alarms
With you by my side you're all, I need
A misty sense of dread
As in the formed silver vase
An empty space beside my chair,
The warming touch of gentle hands
Nothing new to say
I am ready to stop the culture of widows
Let's talk of roses and romance,
So believe in love
We're one and the same.

.

BHANUMATI MISHRA

Death in Banaras

As my soul floats,
over endless oceans
and seamless skies;
four pairs of hairy legs
hurry down narrow lanes,
to rest my lifeless frame
on some limbless trees,
that wait to perish with me.

The 'dom' assures ancestral peace,
salivating dogs howl a welcome;
salvation smiles ever so faintly -
a strange lightness descends on me.
At 'the ghat of the only world',
I see my fidgeting progeny,
saffron shrouds; shrunken eyes;
shaven heads; sweating brows -
feeding crows who proxy me.

As flames leap up to match the sun;
It's time to say a worldly goodbye,
I know you long to go home, my sons,
and turn your backs to where I lie.

DEBENDRA SAHU

Fly like a Butterfly

If I won't forget your sins and forgive you,
Even though I won't recall and recognize
In my next life, with my fresh costumes
I will carry that baggage of wounds,
To be your bigger ravager without
Being aware or even remembering you.
Whenever I will be oaring to propel the boat
A shadow will be emerging intercepting the light
From within the walls of the lake
To ride on my back,
Abide with me all through the day and night
Like ubiquitous, to wither my lamp of spirit.
Someday, when a dream will recur to be a butterfly
And I may also emerge from your pupae,
But I won't be able to fly
Because my wings shall not open,
Wings will take another life to dry and shrivel
And then flutter under the sky,
Hence today let my river of sins with the baggage
Flow into the sea emptying the evil-debts.

EZHIL VENDHAN

I Love My Country India

I love the cultural and philosophical
beauty of my country India.
I love the intellectual heritage,
the folk spread throughout the vast country,
the peasants, the shepherd, the fishing,
and tribes of the forests and hills.

I am proud of the entire
landmass of the subcontinent,
with embodiment of natural beauty.
The Himalayas on the north,
and the Indian Ocean on the south
surrounded by the Arabian sea
and the Bengal ocean.

I enjoy the glacial rivers and long tributaries,
the regions grew fertile over thousands of years.

But I am ashamed of the persisting
ugly caste system, untouchability,
the dowry system of Indian marriage,
the male preference in child birth,
and the dirty dynastic politics prevalent

IRANNII SAIKIA

She Is A Demotic Poet

She is a demotic poet
Within her stolen love or beloved,
Where ideas, thoughts make herself
To think as a prophet.

Without wildness
Peope needs to sail on a sea
And on an ocean within a new route.
Whereas they forgot the substance of sublime.

Standing in a desert
She feel her love of Ice-Berg.
Where destiny shows the review of past,
About frigid, temperate, thorrid and humidity.

Feeling as a demotic
She transforming her community standard
Into a noble heart.
Such as prairies of grassland that converted into the wheat
basket.

A demotic poet becoming a royal and wise,
Where she is ready to transform a mind of humiliation.
Through the sence of demure and humidity.
When her tears had been wiped out by herself.

Thinking of her love of mud
She is climbing the top of hillock.
Where the destiny of a global warming,
Needs to inquest a row into a fire circle.

Feeling as a demotic poet
And without beloved
She is transforming her love to prayer.
Where her loves becoming as a wise and loyal.

JAWEED AHMED

Redemptive Musings

Heed my cute presence
Read my mute silence
Reveal my awaken muse
Anneal my unshaken views
Revere my retentive perceiving
Hear my redemptive musings
Feel my enlightened soul
In my lightened words

JHILAM CHATTARAJ

Celebrations

Holi
My hands
born of one spring
breeze, claim a vivid moon
birthing a fish, in a pool of
red ink

Diwali
Sparks seal
a city's soul.
Fire embroidered sky lit
by a child, burning his father's
bleak breath

Rakhi
I rose
from your veins to
one scarlet thread and a
white grain of rice; borrowed bruises-
brother

Christmas
Carols,
one town of ash
and steel. Sunlit mouths wait
for a woman in a red suit.
Plum fog

KANCHAN YADAV

The Man at Work

I see him daily working at the kiln,
His hands are muddy 24×7.
His ragged brief, drenched in sweat,
Exposes his body parts to the scorching Sun.
But free from worries he is busy in creation
He Moulds bricks with some inscription;
Probably abbreviated name of the owner on it.
The dexterity he shows amazes me;
Dedication to his work is unparalleled.
His smiling face, perhaps masking dejection
Raises doubts and compels me to think:
While Moulding bricks for the houses of others,
Doesn't he desire to Mould for his own?
Perhaps he doesn't give it a second thought
And accepts that he is destined for the makeshift home.

LEENA RAJAN

Patience vs. Luck

River water turns bitter, if we are unlucky,
Reflections like this, are shifty and shaky
Rebuking and blaming fate is naughty,
Rating fate as cause of all is filthy.

Impatience is mostly the cause of falls,
If in composed mode, living is desirable.
In abruptness we aren't prepared to react,
In sufferings, as we lack mature thoughts,

And we can solve nothing, if unprepared,
And, we become down and desperate.
At a dark path, if one leg firmly fixed,
A probe we can, with other leg moved.

Prudence is this, preparations' meaning is,
Prejudging the future situation and dangers,
Perceiving future by any is never possible,
Preparations help us to face any trouble.

Lo! If we are to face hardships in due course,
Let us face them, utilising drafts and plans
Let us tackle issues in hand with prudence,
Loftily planning life's future and success.

MANJULA ASTHANA MAHANTI

Missing

My life is barren without you
Anxiously waiting for you
When will I listen to your words
My sweet treasure
When my heart will get
Respite from eagerness
I'm unable to sleep, long for you,
My diligent eyes looking for you
I know, you are fragile
But embrace me tightly
You are my own, my inspiration
A joyous dream of morning
My pages are blank, empty,
Unable to express, create poetry,
Be with me, my dear, "Imagination "
What kind of emotions, expressions,
Absolutely lost, without you,
O my rescuer, my dear "Artistry"
Stay with me, always...

MOLLY JOSEPH

Tolerance

tolerance is mine when they undermine
my beliefs and revel in ideologies
antithetical to mine..

tolerance comes as let go,
a passive acceptance
of passions spent on matters frivolous...

tolerance is tuning your mind
on the patient wait
for the calm after the storm..

keeping away from the medley,
you long for peace..
tolerance is allowing yourself to be taken for a fool,
a coward, one who shies away from response..

again, just by being there, you are taken as a
clone, following them, shuffling your feet behind.

your self esteem is put to task,
 never mind, your convictions are yours..

to survive in a world,torn between divided ends
tolerance is the one alibi,
 though a difficult pill to take..

MANJU SINGH

Where Peace and Culture Flourish..

O muse ! bless my pen
to sing the glory of
the abode of Lord Shiva
to recite the beauty
of a divine land in whose lap
the knowledge and wisdom flourished ..
Its aura is magnificent
it's holiest pilgrimages of all
bathed in soul stirring hyms all the time
here the day starts with arti of maa Ganga
the pristine look , its fragrant breeze
every bit of it pulsating with art ..
It is land of Tulsi and Raja Harishchandra the great upholder of
truth
It attracted Lord Buddha the saviour of humanity to spread his
teachings
it lured Pandit Madam Mohan Malviya to institute reservoir of
knowledge
it's land of Bismillah Khan ,the king of melodies
it's home of Munshi prem Chand ,
Jayshankar Prasad the great literary luminaries ..
The capital of culture and religion
attracts devotees to God
its seren and soothing view
fills heart with joy
it is believed here human soul is relieved of cycle of death and
birth..

MANTHENA DAMODARA CHARY

Let Me Sing Thy Glory

O Father, allow me to be a flame
To end with equanimity all blame
We,humans,seek temporal fame
Rendering basic standards lame

Let me be a spark to end gloom
Make me a blissful bud in bloom
Thou script one's decisive doom
The sinners never find any room

I long to sing Thy glory in a song
Like a bird with such joy for long
I wish to be a rainbow in the sky
Filling colours in horizon so high

I wish to sing like a lark at length
Giving weak hearts real strength
Let me share my joy with others
Treating them all as my brothers

Then this world will be a heaven
We can not see all worlds seven
Let this birth be full of rare mirth
Cherishing beauties of this earth

MEENAKSHI GOSWAMI

Phoenix

Was it a dream?
When I was alone and spent my days in loneliness
You entered my life giving me joy and happiness..
I dreamt of a jungle full of flowers;
In that dream I touched the moss on some stones
And there appears a Phoenix sitting on a tree
Singing, as if its voice had been filled with agony for years.
Flames were coming from its wings.
When the flames rose higher,
I saw the Phoenix burning in them.
Was this the Dream?
I woke up and felt that the wet moss still clung to my fingers
and feet.
But that was when I realized
That it was I who was the Phoenix !
I saw myself burning and burning
And then burning to ashes.

NEHA KUMARI

Home

This heart
I sense
Is not my home
Always I was
Not a vagabond
I wanted to build
A nest , a home
When I saw a house
I claimed it
As a home of my own
The owner offered me
A pair of keys
One he kept with himself
I kept the next one
From inside I bolted the door
To feel the home
After a while
To see him outside
To call him for the dinner
To walk in the green
I unlatched the door
I couldn't open
I was locked
The person to whom

The heart and home belonged
Was a wanderer
A true adventurer
Thus I knew
A home cages people
You know
From the day
To this minute,
The idea of home scares me
When I see a home
I run fastly
More fastly
For a temporary shelter
Do you know
I always search a home.

OTTERI SELVAKUMAR

Silence Please

The tree laughs in silence
Silence looks at the tree's breath
Silence seems in its life
What does silence belong
To the tree alone?
In the stormy wind, the tree moves silently in silence
You can feel the tranquility...
If you have peace
What is the name of that peace?
Or don't ask me to meditate on it.
It will tell you your intuition
What is the sign of the tree...
Whereas it
Knows the identity of the whisper
The tree loves silence…
If you want to remain silent
Sit under the tree
To your mouth and mind
Put the lock on and leave
About your Silence…

PARAMANANDA MAHANTA

Love lane

My butterfly heart flutters through your door ,
With expansive senses in relentless pour .
The stream of roses from your voice ,
Flow me upstream in a pleasure case.

Reaping your beauty with endless joy
In ripening warmth of sensory ploy.
Forecasted love and uncharted pleasure,
Rendering me deep to divine door.

Bliss of paradise laundering your lane,
Breathing heavily on joyous drain .
Your lipless mouth and lidless eye,
In a devouring mood to unshackle glee .

Unscanned beauty and unfolded love ,
Pinned my heart like a chanting dove.
Flourishing joy for ecstastic pleasure ,
Heaven on earth now gets a door.

PERUGU RAMAKRISHNA

Many Faces

I thought he's just one...
but peeped out from him many a one!
One face behind the veil, one face vulpine
one albunic and one well embellished!
One shady face, chummy with darkness
and one like a double-hooded serpent.
So many faces in one man,
tell so many untold tales.

In his gait soaked in intoxication
yodels of spurious philosophy;
behind his bright sagacious visage
 winking two dark eyes;
and behind the dale of his one candid word
a mountain of lies...
I keep going on in search of a truthful face
amongst these hordes
of multiple lineaments of sanctimony.
Yes...I am still in search of that one face,
one lonely face, as clear as mirror..!

P.S.V.PRASAD BABU

Leave the gun

Oh! terrorist,
Leave your passion gun
Enjoy scarlett of the sun
Remember your mother
Treat everyone as your brother

Leave your blasting bomb
Fulfil desire of your mom
Remind your friends ever
To make life as fabulous forever

Love and like others
With your peace feathers
Fill your blood with kind
To have a peaceful mind.

Don't disturb beautiful nature
To have a fantastic future
Share love to ever green earth
To lead life ever happy and mirth.

PARASHURAM RAO GANDE

The City Of Pearls Comes Alive

In the month of July every year
Unique city comes alive
The Ujjain Mahankali becomes cheerful
In fact all the temples of the Deity Mahankali
Are abuzz with devotees
Festive atmosphere prevails every where
All the temples are decorated with marigold flowers
All the streets are full of processions
All the roads lead to Mahankali temples
The glorious city is a village at once
The rich and poor take part in the festivities grand
The earthen pots full of yellow rice
On the heads of well dressed women devotees
The life of margosa leaves around
The pots and in their hands
The feet of women decorated with turmeric hues
Move towards Kali temples of the city
Amidst sounds of bands and dances
Bhagyanagar is at once a sea of devotees
One simply wonders at the divine aura of deities

RAJBABU GANDHAM

Did you find…?

I am born, I was a child
I went to school, I played in grounds
I broke my bones, I cried a lot
I made friends, I went to movies
I kissed my girls, I got my hurts
I passed college, I got a job
I married a girl, I had dinners
I made love, I have children
I have a house, I own a car
I have money, I lost my parents
I had my responsibilities, I struggled in life
I had failures, I too succeeded
I was joyous, I made merry
I had my celebrations, I travel a lot
I regret nothing, I enjoy living

yet

I haven't found
who is this I

DID YOU?~yathi

RAJUMONI SAIKIA

After all it is a poison

What poison is this ! By which I am gaining pain after pains,
Suffering after sufferings.

What power is this!
By which I am brought
here and there
In the sun and in the rains too.

Oh ! Of course
I am but elated by my feelings who grow my creative horizon
day after days and brought to an another world within me like
an unidentified person.

I am unknown about the clouds of poison growing on my
forehead. Don't know why I am suffering inside this beauty
within and within.

RANJANA SHARAN SINHA

Cathartic Avenue

Trajectory of emotions
 into a starless night,
perceptive patterns
 stir like threads of kite;

Once a figure
 now a silhouette,
a futile linger
 within and without!

The poetic inspirations
 Seem to recede--
My passion and possession
 deep within me!

The avenue of self expression:
 My cathartic outlet
The world of peace and compassion
 never to forget.

Silent secret invisible power,
 stay alive, O stay
in my divine heart's bower,
 Never, Never go away!

RANU UNIYAL

My City is a stranger to me

My city melts
in my arms as I rush
towards the unfamiliar
terracotta streets.

The fibre sticks
and the stumbling dreams
like naphthalene balls
wriggle free from the clutches.

Grinning, the fragrance
stays back and all else
drifts ashore.Have you
noticed the silent sun?

The houses choose
to hide their grief.
Only feet seem desperate
To find a resting place.

RAMESH SINGH

Togetherness

The harsh realities of the world
The will to achieve
The urge to triumph
It is only together
And not alone
That we can succeed
I live for it,
And hope you'll be with me forever
The spiritual power allow to meet us together
Only to create a rare
Combination of elegance
And exclusivity
Let's weave the eternal magic of
Our Friendship, our Love.

RITA DE

A Keen Eye

Self control, inquisitiveness
Complacence and good association
Are the four door-keepers
On the way to attain liberation.
An intelligent seeker
Keeps a keen eye on
How to make friendship
With those four door-keepers
Or at least
One must nurse
One of the four door-keepers in himself.

That is why
Only one or two with halo
Are carved for years
And stand for the pole star
To guide one along the right path

SANGEPU NAGESWARA RAO

Humanity is an Ocean

Every human being has a humanity
Few drops of an ocean are dirty.
Like somebody has not humanity
All the people are living in the society.

Knowledge becomes more cheerful
We need the freedom of wonderful.
To get strength from the city of beautiful
Men and women are enjoying as joyful.

Some words are having a lot of energy
Which are mainly Humanity.
The humanity has a lot of power
It's great responsibility.

To get confidence you should wait and patience
Sometimes we feel insecurity.
It's a lot of ability
It belongs to HUMANITY.
Humanity is an ocean.

Humanity has a love
Humanity has a hope
Humanity has a fear
Humanity has a faith
Love your country like a legend
All are having a lot of HUMANITY.

SHIKHA CHATTERJEE

And Time Went By...

As the placid blue of a summer sky
Descended into the weary eye,
Distances began to melt...
And soon they felt
They were two fiery souls, now silent presences
That needed time and even fences
Against the din of surrounding noise
Of evening park goers – girls and boys.
They would try to grasp those long-lost years
That had dried up their desperate tears.
What cruel fate had wrenched them apart
Locking tumultuous storm in their heart?
In strange destinies engulfed...it wasn't their fault.
Yet chance did make them somersault
Many decades into the 'now'.
Looking around they wondered how
They'd gather the embers of their life
Still glowing beneath torment and strife.
They'd rise from the ashes, subdue their pain
If life would be the same again.

SUNITA PAUL

Growing up

I grew up with
Smell of my mother's hairs
My granny's pampers and care
My disciplined father's strict rules
The prayer bell , morning assembly of my school
Teacher's scoldings and loving lessons
Listening to boring lectures by sleeping with patience
My tiny library of fairy tales , romance or mystery
Hatred of Mathematics and love for English and History
Playing hide and seek with friends
Torturing grandfather and then making amends
Watching the flowers and butterflies
Committing deliberate mistakes and
denying them with white lies
Making castles with cards and drenching in the rain
Wish I could do all again
Lying in maa's lap and cuddling with love
I grew up with all these small things above

VANDITA DHARNI

Quintessential Peace

When our mind is at war with the soul
Each day pierces like a shaft,
Knocking out wisdom to the wind;
Sniffing like a bloodthirsty scavenger
Robbing the mind of all emotions,
Nestled in the womb of devastation,
The mind a labyrinth of wired webs
Waits on the grim edge of the unknown,
Absolutely abandoned and alone.
But let not hope desert us.
Because in the flashes of lightning
An ethereal presence overpowers,
Exceeding peace pervades,
The soul experiences ethereal bliss,
Peace permeates the deepest crevices,
Soothes the fire that rages
Quells the innermost anguish,
Shames the perpetrator of the conflict
Salvaging the broken spirit.
Nurturing it with love, hope and compassion,
Breaking through every delusion.
Peace must be restored at any cost
Or sanity is permanently lost.

VINAMRATA

My Phoenix

Cling to your dreams, create and inspire.
Don't let it turn to ashes on a burning pyre.
In your heart is buried a seed,
Let it not die, take heed.
Fill your heart with light,
Break free from suffocating compartment tight.
Water it with love and care,
Let the seed bloom beyond compare.

Soar high little bird, got wings so fly.
Leaving behind taboos that ask you "Why?"
It will not be easy but do not succumb.
Ideas flow in your veins, Don't be silent and numb.
Leave behind earthly chains and clashes,
My Phoenix rising from its ashes.

VOLIVOJU, SAMMAIAH CHARY

The Miracle of Humanity

Humanity is magical and marvellous word
It can bring hue of compassionate to the world.
Inhumanity is shaped on slyness,
Now we should be abide of prosperous and fairness

Humanity had enormous spirit to keep smile.
But people run with selfishness of sail,
It shall be drowned to us,
Keep generous and away from nervous'

Humanity keeps peace and harmony among humane.
It is essential to our world to shine'
But unfortunately it's fading out to run'
Narrow minds dominate on legacy of humanity

Humanity eases the gap between families and society
And it makes as strong as almighty
So keep humanity for bright
Tender minds of future light

WILLIAMSJI MAVELI

Harvest

Oh, give us pleasure in the flowers to-day;
And give us not to think so far away;
As the uncertain harvest; keep us here
All simply in the springing of the year.
Oh, give us pleasure in the orchard white,
Like nothing else by day, like ghosts by night;
And make us happy in the happy bees,
The swarm dilating round the perfect trees.
And make us happy in the darting bird
That suddenly above the bees is heard,
The meteor that thrusts in with needle bill,
And off a blossom in mid air stands still.
For this is love and nothing else is love,
The which it is reserved for God above
To sanctify to what far ends He will,
But which it only needs that we fulfil.

BINDI SHARMA

Mistakes

The biggest room in the world is the room for improvement

If you feel you have no faults....
There is another one!
If you don't want to learn from
Your mistakes
There is no sense in making them.

Man's mind , once stretched by a new idea
Never regains it's original shape
Are you fit company for the person
You wish to become?
Your thoughts are the architect of your destiny
But what happens to a man is less significant
Than what happens within him

There are times when. Man should be content with what he has
"Santosh paramam Dhanam"
When man finds no peace within himself
It is useless to seek it elsewhere then we won't consider
suggestions ,we reject our own potential
But most important of life's battles is the one
We fight daily in the silence
Of our souls !!

RENETTE DSOUZA

The Voice of Humanity

You inherited me in your mother's womb
For you were born into this world a human
But on the path of a materialistic world
You lost me, in all its chaos and confusion.

Sow me back into the depths of every soul
That I may grow again from within everyone
Make all your lives and spirit whole
Fill it with kindness and compassion.

Like the warmth emitted from the rising sun
Let me bloom tenderness in every eye
To care for the poor and the downtrodden
Into every heart let me breed and multiply.

Let me sprout feelings of love and care
In a world divided by color, religion and race
So you can all learn to provide and share
Believe you can make this world a better place.

Bridled by each other's happiness and not misery
Casting away bitterness, spite and enemity
Under one religion you shall be set free
Let your only religion be me, the religion of Humanity.

ANURADHA BANERJEE

A Corridor of Silence

My songs have entered
a corridor of frozen moments.
A path leading to silence…
endless …
"I can't say when did all this start…,
this process of getting sucked in by silence!"
I confessed to my counsellor
in one of the prolonged sessions.
He tried his best all his techniques-hypnosis even.

His chamber vibrated with digital designs
ready to inject virtual happiness.
I told him: "Shadows of broken nests hover around
thirst synges my being…
mirage of water deludes…
a lump of frozen tears rattles in the throat…."

"Do you ever see children in your dreams?
sparrows? the blue skies?" asked my counsellor eagerly
My tongue wobbled:"Oh! I told you
I have lost my songs,
the nests, the green-everything pristine
Can you retrieve me? Can you redeem?"

My healer gasped I heard him mumble,
"Children! horror…horror… in the prayer hall
in flames, burning… I confess to my sin.
I torched the prayer hall…"

The waves of unleashed sin
choked his voice
He too has entered the corridor of silence.

RACHNA SRIVASTAVA

Sunday afternoon

A day away from work
I lazed around on a Sunday afternoon
Sitting beside a swimming pool
With a book in my hand
And a cool drink by my side
Ah! The perfect setting
I remembered my childhood days
When a Sunday afternoon meant oiling your hair and sit with
mother
Smelling the delicacies being cooked in the kitchen
No worry in life except the tests and exams
Mother and father forming a security bank
Gone are the days
When brothers and sisters would sit together and do mundane
things
Gone are the days long ago
Now only a thing to reminisce
Sitting beside the pool
I remember those days.

BINA SINGH

She

Dark holds no terror
The binding vines are loose
The shutters are pulled down
Although thin, yet the silvery rays
Are filtering in

The ashes don't cover anymore
Like Phoenix, she has risen
Opening the wings
Fluttering, soaring to reach the blue

The chirupping birds above
The gurgling currents beneath
Alluring, inviting, stirring
Stimulated, she bleeds
Moves to embrace the serene invitation

Thus, floating, breaking the temporal barriers
SHE joins the rolling melody.

PURNIMA SINGH

Shattered to Pieces

Hot summer afternoon and burning fire,
The red and yellow snakes of flames,
Rose from the funeral pyre
The smoke was burning, the burning eyes
The eyes lose vision, it cries
And with force my hand tries
To hit hard on my grandfather's skull
To break it down to pieces
So that the body is completely burned
         The skull shatters into pieces
          And I look at the open skull
          My soul shrieks, my body freezes
My body freezes in the afternoon Sun
I can't see and yet I see
The charred body and the shattered brain
The brain helping me solve mathematics
         The brain mapping unknown territories
         The cerebrum and cerebellum lay bared
And the brain which was so sharp to act
Lay lifeless and couldn't react.

SUPRIYA SINGH

My Lost Poem

I lost one of my poems
Somewhere within me,
Yesterday, I sensed a trace of it
While preparing tiffin for my son,
It was seen again, thrown with utter carelessness
While making bed of my mother-in-law,
Once again, I tried for its whereabouts
While bathing in haste, but in vain
Though half-heartedly, yet I attempted again
While returning from the office
Tired, I postponed it for tomorrow, a holiday,
The next day, I searched it again
While dusting, cooking and washing clothes,
Alas! The fate didn't favour me
It was completely lost, lost within me,
Another poem died before its birth
Because of shortage of time and space.

कमला पाण्डेय

कैसी संवेदना भेजी

कैसी संवेदना जगी हे मुनीवर! तेरे मन में,
क्रौंचमिथुन को कामकेलिरत देख मनोहर वन में।
हाय व्याध ने मारबाण क्रूरता दिखाई क्षण में,
छटपट करते प्राण विहग के उड़े पवन के संग में।।

क्रौंची ने क्रन्दन से कम्पन भरा विपिन के कण में,
तभी तुम्हारा शोक फूटकर मुखरित हुआ वदन में।
हे निषाद! तुम कभी प्रतिष्ठा न पाना जीवन में,
हुई प्रस्फुटित पहली कविता तब ऋषिवर संस्कृत में।।

फिरी मैथिली वन–वन में,
राघव की व्यथा भवन में!
वही वेदना तुमने कविवर! भेजी मेरे मन में।
अमृतधार पीयूषवाहिनी गंगा के रक्षण में,

हमसे नराधमों ने पाटा कूड़ा उसके तन में,
सिसक रही बन्दिनी बांध के कारा बने सदन में।
इसी शोक में डूबा मन श्लोकायित हो क्रन्दन में,
कहता भागीरथी बहे कैसे भू के आंगन में।।

आशा यादव

सच होते सपने

क्या सोचा था किसी ने कभी
कि मिट्टी से लिपे-पुते आँगन से सटे चौके में
सरकंडों की आग से निकलते धुएँ में
परिवार के लिए बटलोही भर चावल पकाती
माँ की आँखों से बहते आँसुओं में छुपा दर्द
चुभ जाएगा दंश बनकर चुल्हानी की मटमैली ज़मीन में
गुड्डे गुड़ियों का खेल खेलती कलावती के जेहन में एक दिन
और मिटा देगा उसके मासूम दिमाग की धुंध
बनाकर उसे बड़ा छोटी सी उम्र में।
कि लाँघ जाएगी वह घर की चौहद्दी
नाप लेने के लिये दूरी पाठशालाओं की
होने के लिये बड़ी समय से पहले।
कि उठा लेगी दायित्व पूरे परिवार का
मजबूत कंधों पर अपने।
हो जाएगी तैयार खड़ी होने को हजार अन्य कलावतियों के साथ
कि भर देगी अदम्य ऊर्जा उनके भी पंखों में।
उड़ने लगेंगी वे भी अपने मजबूत डैनों को पसार
ऊँचे आसमान में क्षितिज के उस पार।
क्या सोचा था किसी ने कभी कि सिखा देगी वह उन्हें भी
संवेदना के सूत्र को पकड़ने की कला
बड़ी मजबूती से जड़ों से अपनी जुड़ी रहने के साथ।
कि फिर कभी किसी भी माँ की आँखों से
बेसमय छलकते आँसुओं का दर्द
न चुभे दंश बन किसी की नन्हीं सी जान को।
कि न छिने किसी कलावती का फिर से बचपन गुड़ियों से खेलने की कच्ची सी उम्र में।

सच बिल्कुल सच
क्या सोचा था कभी भी किसी ने
बड़ी शिद्दत से पूरे होते
कलावती के जेहन में बुने जाते हुए इस सपने का सच

बानीब्रत महन्ता

आज़ादी

हर भूखा भूख से आजाद हो और हर अखबार झूठ से आजाद हो।

आस्था हर उन्माद से आजाद हो और गरीब अपनी गुरबत से आजाद हो

खुली हवा में साँस लेने को सब आजाद हों।

लाल रंग सरहदों या मुहल्लों में नहीं

बल्कि शाम के डूबते सूरज में किसी की उतरती हिना में और किसी बच्चे के गुब्बारे में चमकता हो।

हमारे खेतों के रंग और हरे हों।

किसान को भी किसी गोल सी दिखती रस्सी पर अपने बच्चे का झूला टांगने की आजादी हो।

नफरतों की हर एक कहानी सूली चढ़ जाए

और हर एक मोहब्बत का फ़साना आजाद हो।

शान्ता चटर्जी

जलाऊंगी एक दीप

किसी ने कहा तो था–''आई है ऋतु शरद की''
पर मेरे धूल भरे आँचल में काश के फूल कहाँ खिले?
जब धूँधले से आसमान में–चमके नहीं रातभर तारे–
मने के हरसिंगार के फूल मेरे माथे पर कहाँ गिरे?
फिर भी जलाऊंगी एक दीप तुम्हारे लिये।
बरसात ने बहुत पहले ही समेट लिया था–
अपने लटों को एक तरफ,
कहीं वह गयी, कहीं सूखी ही रह गयी है–
सराबोर कहाँ हुई रस से?
फिर भी जलाऊंगी एक दीप–तुम्हारे लिए।
सूखती हुई गंगा की पतली–सी धार में–
कहाँ लौटा कलरव राजहंसों का?
आकाश को भेदते हुए बहुतल भवनों की भीड़ में–
देखा है किसी ने उठाकर आँख सरसों को?
मैं तो गौरैया भी खोज रही हूँ।
फिर भी जलाऊंगी एक दीप–तुम्हारे लिए।
डूब रहा अंधेरे में सूरज,
धूल और धूएँ में खो रही है चाँदनी और चाँद भी,
बजी कहाँ बाँसुरी रास की?
चकवे का छोटा सा जोड़ा कहाँ खोया?
यमुना का छोर कहाँ मिले?
फिर भी जलाऊंगी एक दीप–सदियों से सदियों तक तुम्हारे लिये।

नैरंजना श्रीवास्तव

पसरी हथेली

पाया कैसा तन
खुला यूँ बेवजह।
तपती अगन में,
ज्यों पिघलता काँच हो।
संघर्ष करती,
ढाँकने को किसलिए।
आँधी ग़रीबी की,
उड़ाती लाज हो।
मरती नहीं हूँ शर्म से,
माँ हूँ बनी,
बच्चे जिलाती,
दूध करके प्राण को।
मेरी तड़प,
होगा तमाशा और का।
अपने लिए,
हर दिन लड़ाई आप हूँ।
इन कालतम हाथों में
न हों रेख, पर,
पसरी हथेली,
ज़िंदगी का नाम हूँ।।

मंजू कुमारी

राणा को प्रणाम

भारतभू के अमर सिपाही!
शत शत मेरा तूझे प्रणाम।
जिनके कुल में जनम लिये तुम
वे पुरखे थे बड़े महान।
जिस जननी ने जनम दिया था
उसके दूध को दिया सम्मान।।
जिसके रज में चले बढ़े तुम
उस धरती को करुं प्रणाम।।
जिस रमणी का वरण किया था
वन.वन उसने किया प्रयाण।
धन्य धरा वह समरभूमि की
लड़े जहा। तुम समर महान।।
सुखलोलुप इस जन पयोधि में
तुझ सा दीपक नहीं सुजान।
पुनरूउठो तलवार उठा लो
भ्रष्टजनों से हमें दो त्राण।।
घासों की रोटी के स्वाद का
उनसे कर दो नवल बखान।
एक बार फिर सीखें जन.जन
सुख अनन्त देता बलिदान।।

AUTHOR BIO

Aneeta Chitale

Aneeta has been travelling since she was two years old as her father was in the Indian Army. The challenges of her early life has given her many opportunities, to grow and shine as she paved her way into her adult life. As a kid she has changed ten schools, lead a total nomads life. She started writing poems since ten. Many of her poems are published in International Journals. Nature has always fascinated her. She pursues an eclectic style in her penmanship. She is a versatile persona and has acted in a 'Marathi' Movie when she was just 20 year's old and offered a movie by the Film an Television

After graduating from Pune University, she made her career as an educator. She has worked in India and overseas. She loves working with children. She has recently published her debut novel "Sojourn To Maldives". She has worked in Maldives, Dubai and UK. She has made her foray in the writing world, by penning her novel on the international relations.

Antonio J Rivas Melean

Antonio J Rivas Melean. Poet and author of several publications. Member of many organizations and groups of poets locally and worldwide. Venezuelan, retired, engineer and scientific researcher and an author. Actual publishes in the academy -edu., of the National Academy of Sciences of the United States. He is an engineer, former engineering professor at the University of Carabobo, a former teaching assistant at the Central University. He has a long curriculum as a professional in engineering, former teaching, management, business man promoter, scientific research and courses at international levels in different countries.

George Onsy

George Onsy (b. 1953) an Egyptian thinker, poet and artist, is a Professor of English and Art-architecture History at The Egyptian-Russian University, Cairo and other academies. His outstanding works of poetry and art calling for a universal unifying spirituality have been published in several international printed anthologies, magazines and e-zines. He is a recipient of several awards notably "The Global Icon of Peace Award"-2017 and "The Most Outstanding Peace Poet-2017" - 2018 (Nigeria) and "The Best Poet Award"-2017 (World Nation Writers Union, Kazakhstan). At present, he is the Secretary General of the INTERNATIONAL HIGHER ACADEMIC COUNCIL OF ENGLISH LITERATURE (IHACEL). He has received the Honorary Certificate of THE LIVING LEGEND OF THE 20TH CENTURY from the same organization in April 2019.

His poems have been published in more than 40 international anthologies and featured in poetry magazines and broadcast in different countries. His works have also been translated into different international languages like Telugu, Odia, for India as well as Chinese, Greek, Italian, Spanish. He himself also writes poetry, in Arabic, French, Spanish, Italian, German and Russian beside English. George Onsy has been lately nominated by many thinkers, writers and conference organizers round the world for Nobel Prize.

Isah Wisdom

Isah Wisdom known by the pen name Wisdom Wise Wonder is a teacher, writer and poet. Since 2013 he has written over a hundred poems on different themes such as nature,love, happiness and healing. His goal is simply to use poetry as a medium to spread the message of love. He currently teaches English at CleverMinds school and lives in Warri, Nigeria.

Jyotirmaya Thakur

Author of fifteen original Poetry books, World Poet Laureate, Living legend of 21st century,Peace Icon and HPAW Ambassador of Humanity ,Jyotirmaya Thakur is the first Indian born poetess to be published by Real Vision Aspirant Writers Publication,UK. An award winning author and poet ,she has served as a Vice -Principal (retired) of an International school in India, an editor, reviewer, researcher, columnist,public speaker, Reiki Master , Spiritual and Social activist. She is the President of Chamber of Poets and Vice President of the World Parliament of literature of World Union of Poets of Italy. National Director of Public Relations and Communications of Union Hispano Mundial de Escritores ,Peru,in India . 'Universal Ambassador of Culture' for Writers and Artist union of Bolivia approved by UNESCO. The title of 'HONOURED POET Of INDIA -by Seychelles Government accredited - International Literary and Art society 'Lasosyasyon Lar San Frontyer (LLSF). 'World Poetic Star' certificate of Diploma by WNWU- Kazakhstan.

Chief counsellor of Telangana Poetry forum and an executive member of the educational magazine LITERATI and a columnist. An editor of various magazines and Anthologies .She is a member of Wolf International Poetry Exhibition group of UK, where her poems are exhibited in various art galleries, Literary clubs and public places . She has been featured among the"Woman of Essence" by dotism magazine, Australia and as one of the "Woman of Substance " anthology by World Pictorial Poetry forum.

Mary Lynn Luiz

Mary Lynn Luiz was born May 15th, 1945 in USA, State of Florida. Graduated Auburndale High School in 1964, Studied Philosophy, Psychology, Sociology, and Ethics at Polk State College 1978 through 1989. Retired Branch Manager of Sunniland Corporation 1971 – 2001. Lived in Dubai UAE 2001 – 2005. Lived in Alexandria Egypt 2005 – 2010.
She began writing poetry in 2014 under the encouragement of Satya Pattnaik , from Odessa India, University President and Poet. Recently retired 2019. She has had several of her poems translated into different languages and published in several anthologies, magazines, and books over the world! Her first work is, "Do Not Sell The Spring" which she edited, and wrote the foreword for, and helped to design the cover. Her poems continue to be published in many different venues. She was appointed by World Union of Poets as Director for the State of Florida, USA. Until she resigned that post. She has received several awards from poetry clubs and organization. She has been featured on The John Kavanagh Show, Poetry for Peace YouTube with her poetry set to music, for the poems "You Make The Sun to Shine Again", and "Dance Forevermore". She has published two e-books of poetry titled "Wisdom Whispers" on September 25th 2018 and on April 2nd 2019 published "Wisdom Whispers Poetry". And now "Wisdom In Pearls of Poetry" August 05, 2019. She has three other e-books that will be published in the near future! She received The Gold Star Award

from Literature Lovers Association for her Haiku Poem in Micro poetry, World of Poetry and Prose Award for Poetic Excellence. She was rated the 2nd best poet in the world for the second quarter of 2019 by The Best Poet or Poetess of the World Poetry Group.

Muhammad Shanazar

Muhammad Shanazar is a poet from Pakistan, he is a recipient of Universal Inspirational Poet, World Icon of Peace, The International Best Translator 2012, 1st Four Stars Ambassador in the World, Naji Naaman Literary Laureate Prize 2015, Extraordinary Ambassador for Gratis Culture, Poet of the World, Cross for Peace, Cross for Literature, Pride of Pakistan, Herbert Macaulay Award, World Laureate in Literature 2017, Pride of the Globe, Literaurnost Gold Award, The World Best Poet 2017, Pride of the Globe 2017, Ambassador of Humanity, Poetic Galaxy Award, Ambassador of Justice and Peace, Ambassador De Literature, Connoisseur De Poetry 2018, one of The Best Six Writers of the World, recognized by UNESCO, Noble Star for Literature 2018, Global Literature Guardian Award 2018, The World's Most Inspirational Writer's Award, World Icon of Literature, World Ambassador of Literature, Temirqazyq The Best Poet of The World 2018, Master of War Imagery, Global Doves of Peace, Honoured Poet of Pakistan and several others. He had been the Secretary General of World Institute for Peace Nigeria, 2nd Secretary General of World Union of Poets, Italy and the First Vice President of World Nations Writers' Union Kazakhtan.

Shahid Abbas

Shahid Abbas, a poet in the English language, a story teller and opinion writer from Tandlianwala (karpala) Faisalabad Pakistan.

Tariq Muhammad

Tariq Muhammad is a bilingual poet writing under the pseudonym M. Tariq. Writing poetry in English, Hindi and Urdu, with English as the primary language. Hailing from Kolkata, WB, he now resides in America. His debut poetic work, MUMTAZ. The Making Of The Taj Mahal is a self published book on a single topic as how The Taj Mahal came into being. His current voluminous book on the verge of completion is an epic story on the twenty five Abrahamic Prophets who have influenced the world with their lives work.

Maja Herman Sekulić

Maja Herman Sekulić is an internationally acclaimed author of 17 books. She did her Ph.D from Princeton University, USA and is a Fulbright scholar. She is also a member of Academy of American Poets

Selvam V. Pujari

Dr. Selvam V. Pujari PhD. lives in Itahari, Nepal. He is an Indian Diaspora writer in Poem. This is his first choice in his writing career from 2004 since his university days. He is basically a Dhakshina Bharathiyan from Tamilnadu. He teaches English. He has a PhD in English, from 2015. As of now he has obtained nearly 8 years of teaching in Bharath, Zambia and in Nepal. His dream is to be the National Poet of Bharath, in English.

Anchal Rana

My name is Anchal Rana. I am 17 years old and currently pursuing my studies at CHRIST (Deemed to be a University) Bangalore. I am a journalism and literature student. I've always had an fascination towards literature and poetry . I've written numerous poems to pour out my heart. I don't follow any particular rhyme scheme instead I let my feelings flow with words. I've written this poem 'DEATH SAYS' . It projects death's perception on the world we live in today.

Priya S. Bhardwaj

Priya is a budding poetess. She has completed her BA and MA in English from Banaras Hindu University. Literature is her passion. She always looks out for different opportunities where she can learn and write about new experiences.

Sudeep Sen

Sudeep Sen is a major writer of the contemporary age and has several publication to his credit including *Postmarked India: New & Selected Poems* (HarperCollins), *Fractals: New & Selected Poems | Translations 1980-2015 and Kaifi Azmi: Poems | Nazms (Bloomsbury). He has also edited important anthologies and is recipient of the prestigious* Pleiades' honour for his contribution to contemporary world poetry from Macedonia. Many of his articles and reviews have been published in National and International journals. He is the first Asian honoured to read his poetry and deliver the Derek Walcott Lecture at the Nobel Laureate Festival. The Government of India's Ministry of Culture has awarded him the senior fellowship for "outstanding persons in the field of culture/literature".

Jernail Singh Anand

Dr Jernail Singh Anand (President, World Poetry Conference, India 13-14th Oct 2019) obtained his Ph.D Degree from Punjab University, Chandigarh and is an internationally acknowledged Indian poet, philosopher, spiritualist and scholar. He was honoured with D.Litt. degree by Univ. of South America. He has to his credit more than 60 books of English poetry, prose, fiction, nonfiction and spirituality. He has innovated the theory of BIOTEXT(along with Iranian scholar Dr Roghayeh Farsi) and CLOUD SYNDROME in Critical theory and is a refereed author. His mini-epic 'Geet: The Song Eternal', a sequel to Milton's 'Paradise Lost' , earned rave previews which is running into 2nd edition Geet: THE Unsung Song of Eternity. His major writings include The Ganterbury Tales, a modern sequel to the great Canterbury Tales, 'The Satanic Empire)' (an epic) a sequel to Dante's 'The Divine Comedy', followed by verse anthologies like 'Fighting the Flames' and 'Voices from the Void'. 'The Barbed Wire' (a novel) and 'Facing It' (poetry) are coming up. His works of spirituality 'Bliss:The Ultimate Magic' and 'I Belong to You' have been translated into Persian and published in Iran. He is the recipient of several awards and honours such as Cross of Literature, [World Union of Poets Italy], World Icon of Peace [Nigeria] etc.

Anil Deshwal Dash

Dash is a marine engineer, a seaman by profession.Deeply engrossed in fantasy world smitten by charm of deep oceans rivers.Hailing from rural backdrop of village Ladhot District Rohtak Haryana.Parents Dr Dharampal Deswal and Mrs Sukhdevi Deswal. Gained by inheritance writing from his PHD father retired College principal Dr Dharampal Deswal.In tune and harmony with mother nature and fellow living beings.Compassionate and emotive Dash touches cords of internal turmoil. Love is in giving sharing existing together peacefully. Life is in moments, is now. Mysteries shroud us all around marking life worthwhile.

Ankita Pathak

Ankita Pathak is student of M.A. Part I, in Arya Mahila PG College, affiliated to Banaras Hindu University

Arindam Roy

Arindam Roy has 38-year experience in various newsrooms. He was the Managing Editor of a reputed Gurgaon-based Citizen Journalist portal and has held senior positions in several publications. He has contributed 13 chapters to various publications. Of these, seven chapters were published in two Coffee Table Books, published by the Times Group. He is a co-author of a novel, *Rivers Run Back*. He lives in two cities, Allahabad and Bangalore.

Aruna Sri Medipally

Aruna Sri Medipally is a Physics teacher from Hyderabad, Telangana State.India . Poetry is her passion.Her maternal grand father Telkapally Rama Chandra Shasthri was Sanskrit scholar and poet Guru of great VishwanathaSathyanarayana Telugu writer at Bandaru College Machilipatnam. She did her Masters in Mathematics,Psychology , MA English Language and literature .She is author of three poetry books My Muse ,Mystical Anklets and Mosaic Mirror and One Anthology, My Tears.

Bhagirath Chowdhary

Sri Bhagirath Chaudhary is a Poet, writer, philanthropist, global, literary activist, humanist, World Peace Activist, Environment Activist.

Binay Laha

Binay Laha is the editor of Indology magazine. He has authored eight books and received many awards and felicitations. He is from Raiganj, West Bengal.

Brajesh Kumar Gupta "Mewadev"

Brajesh Kumar Gupta is Assistant Professor at Eklavya PG College, Banda, and is a bilingual poet writing in Hindi and English. He also writes novels and short stories. He has received several National, International Awards and Honours.

Bhanumati Mishra

Bhanumati Mishra teaches English Literature at Arya Mahila Post Graduate College, Banaras Hindu University. She is a writer, translator, painter and poet. Her articles, book reviews, poems and translations have appeared in TBR, Critical Flame, Ashvamegh, Cha: An Asian Literary Journal, Muse India and Nether. She is a regular contributor to The Hindu and Hindustan Times. She has authored three books titled Amitav Ghosh and his Oeuvre (2011) and Echoes of Silence - a collection of short stories (2017), & The Crimson Dot: A collection of poems (2018). They are available on Amazon.com. Her areas of interest include post-colonial texts, feminist poetry, historical fiction and partition literature.

Debendra Sahu

A Corporate-Finance professional, since superannuated from UCO Bank as Chief Manager from Mumbai and floated into writing, particularly poems and short stories in English. In the past, his passion for bilingual writing in Odiya and English got recognized through publications of poetries/short stories in magazines, plays in All India Radio, TV and stage. His recent Short stories and poems have been published in various national/International Anthologies/journals including Share of Love, Coffee Table Anthology of Feel Poetry, IPA (ICMDR) 2019, Awareness, Cherry Blossoms, Versatile Verses, Nostalgia, Holistic Healings of Widows, International Anthology of Poems on Autism, Re-Verse the Rivers, Quilled by Patriotism, Namaste Ink, Pictorial Poetry Anthology Just Love Me etc., e-published in Story Mirror, Best Poetry and SETU from Pittsburgh, USA. He has been awarded virtual prizes by Prose and Pictures in competitions. A dreamer by nature, free bird by spirit and seeker by choice is a passionate Writer, who finds his calling in penning down poems and stories through his experience and imagination put together in the best combination. Besides, he is a decent gardener.

Ezhil Vendhan

Ezhil Vendhan is winner of Best Poet of the World 2017 and World Laureate in Literature awarded by World Nations Writers Union, Kazakhstan. He is the founder president of Global Vision Poetry and associated himself with many international literary organisations. He is Vice President of World Nations Writers Union and the President of South India chapter of World Union of Poets. His poems have been translated into twenty five global languages including Chinese and Spanish. His name finds place in the National Panel of Indian Republic Day National Poets since 1995. His poem on Banyan Tree, the National Tree of India, originally written in Tamil in 1991 was the best poem from the classical language Tamil for the Indian Republic Day Multilingual National Symposium of Poets- 1995. He is author of five published books in English, French, Tamil and Azerbaijani.

Irannii Saikia

Iranni Saikia is a teacher by profession. She is a painter a painter as well as a poet and has many published poems to her credit. She has received many awards and certificates from National and International Organization. At present she is Governor of the Disciplinary and Control Bodies of Workd Union of Poets.

Jaweed Ahmed

Jaweed Ahmed is an versatile English Poet from Hyderabad who has written more than three thousand poems and numerous articles so far. Many of his works have been published in National and International Magazines and Anthologies. He has also published his own books " Peerless Pearls " and "Precious Jades". He is known for his lucid style.

Jhilam Chattaraj

Jhilam Chattaraj is an Assistant Professor at R.B.V.R.R Women'sCollege, Department of English, Hyderabad, India.She has authored the books,*CorporateFiction: Popular Culture and the New Writers* (2018) and the poetry collection*When Lovers Leave and Poetry Stays* (2018). Her works have been published in journals like *The Colorado Review, World Literature Today, Asian Cha, Frontier poetry, Voice and Verse Poetry Magazine and The Pangolin Review* among others. She received the CTI excellence award in "Literature and Soft Skills Development", 2019 from the Council for Transforming India and the Department of Language and Culture, Government of Telangana.

Kanchan Yadav

Asst. Professor (Ad-hoc), Dept. of English, Arya Mahila P G College, Chetganj,Varanasi.

Leena Rajan

Leena Rajan, a graduate in Physics and Education and Post graduate in English and Education, is a poet, mostly concerned with mystic love, in constant communion with the Oversoul. Her knowledge of physics and other branches of science, helps her to explore everything scientifically. Besides, she is a painting artist, a violinist and a singer.... Born of late Er. K . Neelakantan, a pioneer Engineer of India and late Mrs. Kavu Neelakantan, in Ernakulam district of Kerala, Mrs. Leena Rajan, has a fervour for English literature and Mathematics from early childhood. She got admission to Govt. Engineering college. But fearing ragging, she had to quit that coveted course. After that what all things she does, seems to be both a compensation for the lost chance and a fulfillment of her soul's rejoicing.

Manjula Asthana Mahanti

Postgraduate in Hindi and Sociology .Graduation... With English hons. B. Ed. Sangeet Prabhakar.. Vocal. Guided postgraduation students. Joined College as senior lecturer. Last worked as school principal. Published... Abhishap Damini Ka.. Translation; Safar ME Dhoop To Hogi..; Kaagaz ki kashti ..Iztiraab gazal sangrah.. '; Unnayan -ek drishtikon... Novel; A collection of Short stories, coming shortly .Submitted my poems in many upcoming International Anthologies. Few of them have come also just as.. Nostalgia.. 3 poems, 1 short story; Voice of Humanity.. 1 poem; Holistic Heelings.. 1 poem; OPA.. 3 poems; ICMDR.... 1 article.Quilled with Patriotism.. 3poems; Recipient of Bharat Ratna Atal Behari; Bajpai Award along with other many Samman.

Molly Joseph

Molly Joseph had her Doctorate in post war American poetry. She retired as the H.O.D., Department of English, St.Xavier's College, Aluva, Kerala, and now works as Professor, Communicative English at FISAT, She writes travelogues, poems and short stories.(for children) has published seven books of poems - Aching Melodies, December Dews, Autumn Leaves, Myna's Musings, Firefly Flickers, It rains, The bird with Wings of Fire and Hidumbi (a translation from Malayalam). She is a poet columnist in Spill Words, Literary Vibes and MAG, the international online Journals and Magazine. She has been awarded Pratibha Samarppanam by Kerala State Pensioners Union, Kala Prathibha by Chithrasala Film Society, Kerala and Prathibha Puraskaram by Aksharasthree, Malayalam group of poets, Kerala, in 2018 . Dr.Molly Joseph has been conferred Poiesis Award of Honour as one of the International Juries in the international award ceremonies conducted by Poiesis Online.com at Bangalore on May 20th, 2018. Her two new books were released at the reputed KISTRECH international Festival of Poetry in Kenya conducted at KISII University by the Deputy Ambassador of Israel His Excellency Eyal David. .Dr. Molly's interests lie primarily in Poetry both Malayalam and English that deals with contemporary issues (like, Nature and gender exploitation, need for more of space for women writing, travel literature and Children's Writing.

Manju Singh

Manju Singh belongs to Varanasi, the Cultural City of India. She holds the post of principal in an aided college of District Sitapur in UP. She has graduated from Punjab University. She has done her masters in English from Purvanchal University, Jaunpur UP and in Education from Awadh University, Ayodhya UP. She is a bilingual and a good orator. For her poetry is the expression of soul and the best way of touching lives. She is great worshipper of nature. She believes that without nature there is no poetry. In her poetry she portrays nature in different shades. For the moon she has great fascination. Apart from that she has written hundreds of poems in spontaneous artistic style. Her soulful and evocative imageries are superb.

Manthena Damodara Chary

Manthena Damodara Chary is the Founder Chairman of Telangana Group of Poetry Forums. He was born at Yelukurthy Haveli in Warangal Rural District of Telangana. He was influenced by his poet mother, Mrs. Manthena Ranga Nayakamma during his boyhood. He has many publications to his credit.He won many awards for his poetry.He has organised two poetry festivals in Hyderabad and brought out ten international anthologies.

Meenakshi Goswami

Meenakshi Goswami is the Principal of CNS HS School, Sonitpur Assam. She writes poetry, short stories and articles for all the leading dailies of North East India and Natinal journals and magazines of India. Her debut of poems "The Sensuous Zephyr" was launched in Melbourne in 2014, where she was invited for poetry session. She is a recipient of State Award for Teachers on 5th September 2014,2015 and 2018 from Govt of Assam and Republic Day Award in 2013 and 2019 for her dedicated service to human resources, Art and Culture. She is also the recipient of Oil Shikshya Ratna Puraskar 2016 in recognition of all round excellence as an educationist. She has attended many multilingual international poetry festivals in India and abroad.

Neha Kumari

The poetess is a research fellow in Banaras Hindu University. She is a native of state Bihar. Being a bilingual poet, she writes both in Hindi and English. She loves to write about all the raw experiences life offers her every day. She calls herself, a prosaic poet.

Otteri Selvakumar

Otteri Selvakumar is a Tamil poet who writes Haiku poems in English. He has seven published books on poetry to his credit. He has been bestowed thirteen awards for his contribution to the field of literature.

Paramananda Mahanta

A teacher in School and Mass Education department of Govt. Of Odisha. A lover of nature and human values and peace .

Perugu Ramakrishna

Perugu Ramakrishna is an International Poet, Translator and Editor. Recipient of AP State Government Best poet award ,Excellence in poetry award from GREECE and Japan in World Congress of Poets organised by UNESCO recognised WAAC. Pulara -8 Medallion Award from Malaysia, World Icon of Peace Award from Nigeria, Poet Laureate from Brazil,

Platinum Cross award from World Union of Poets,Italy, Life time achievement award from Philippines,IWA Bogdani - Humanitarian Poet award from Belgium,World Laureate of Literature award from Khazakisthan,Academy of Latin American Honor from Mexico are some greater achievements of recent time besides about 100 prestigious National awards.

P.S.V.Prasad Babu

P.S.V.Prasad Babu has been working as School Assistant (Eng) at Govt.High School,Medarabasti, Kothagudem, Bhadradri – Kothagudem Dist,Telangana State. He has three Master Degrees in English, Economics and Education from Kakatiya university, Warangal. And qualified APSET in Economics subject in the year 2014. He has 10 years teaching experience in English subject for high school level. His hobbies are writing letters to editors for English news papers on current issues, writing poetry and short stories too.

Parashuram Rao Gande

Parashuram Rao Gande, Former Head Dept. of English, Govt. SRR Degree College, Karimnagar. His poems have been published in Anthologies like The Fancy Realm, Symphony of Peace, Tranquil Muse, A New Beginning, Spring, Window to Peace, Symphony of Souls, Ambrosia, Petals of Peace and Versatile Verses etc. honoured with The Enchanting Muse Award in International Poetry Festival, Hyderabad.

Rajbabu Gandham

Rajbabu Gandham, MBA., MA (English), a multi-lingual poet, a trainer of pranayama and meditation,has been writing poetry since his school days.His poems published in 30 Anthologies . His poem won 3rd place is a contest held by World Union of Poets in 2016.Hewon an Award in " Rabindranath Tagore International Poetry Competition"in 2018 . Conferred KAVYA RATNA award by Literati Cosmos Society in 2018. He won 1stPrize in an International Poetry Contest held by "Citta del Galateo " of ITALY in 2019 . He participated in several National and International Poetry Meets all over India and received medals and certificates. His book of micro poems " pebbles " released recently and planned to release three more books by the end of year 2019.

Rajumoni Saikia

Rajumoni Saikia of Assam , is a multilingual poet. He writes his poems in english, hindi, assamese and bangoli language. He is an author of 16 books. He is a popular poet in assamese language. Already he has received 'Sahitya piyus' award for hindi poetry. Received prestigious 'prerona' award from assam sahitya sabha. Received NEBCUS award fror his literary work.
He is also a drama artist. Received national level 'Natyashree 'awad from alahabad natyasangha, received 'Natyaratna' award fron Andhra Pradesh

Ranjana Sharan Sinha

Former professor of English at S B.City College, Nagpur(MH), Dr.Ranjana Sharan Sinha is a well- known voice in the contemporary Indian Poetry in English. Her poems are prescribed at postgraduate level and have been translated into German, Albanian and Hindi languages.Honoured with many prestigious awards for her contribution to literature. Received accolade from the former President of India, A P.J. Abdul Kalam for her poem 'Mother Nature'.She is an eminent author and literary critic, too.Her poems, short stories, articles and research papers have been featured widely in print and digital publications in dailies, magazines, e-zines, archives and journals including Sahitya Akademi's ' Indian Literature'. Authored and published 07 books in different genres and 50 research papers. Poems published in more than 15 highly scclaimed global anthologies.Research supervisor, RTM Nagpur University, Nagpur. Associated with many literary organizations and Poetry groups.Writes in Hindi, too.

Ranu Uniyal

Ranu Uniyal is Professor of English at Lucknow University. An author of six books, her articles and book reviews have been published widely. Her poetry has appeared in Mascara Literary Review (Australia), Jaggery, Medulla Review, Sketch Book, Twenty 20, Whispers (USA), Littlewood Press (UK), Bengal Lights (Bangla Desh), Asia Literary Review, Cha (Hongkong), The Enchanting Verses Literary Review, Dhauli Review, Muse India, Kavya Bharati, Femina, Manushi, Indian Literature and several anthologies both in India and abroad. She has published three poetry collections: **Across the Divide (2006), December**

Poems (2012) and the most recent **The Day We Went Strawberry Pickingin Scarborough** (2018). Her poems have been translated in Hindi, Oriya, Malayalam, Urdu and Uzbek languages. She also writes poetry in Hindi. She is a founding member of a day care centre for children with special needs in Lucknow.

Ramesh Singh

Ramesh Singh is a Research Scholar in the Department of English, Banaras Hindu University, Varanasi, pursuing his research on the topic "The Select Writings of Dhruba Hazarika, Mamang Dai and Arup Kumar Dutta; An Ecocritical Perspective". He has also worked as a Project Fellow for a UGC sponsored project on "Marginality, Cultural Identity and Deconstruction of History: A Postcolonial Reading of V.S. Naipaul's Novels, Travel Writings and Short Stories". He has presented papers in various national and international seminars. He has worked as a Translation Officer in Defence Accounts Department, Lucknow. Currently he is working as a Hindi Translator in Rajbhasha Cell, Banaras Hindu University.

Rita De

Literary works- Published books of poems, short stories, essays- 20 Survey works on village, silk industry, Ivory works etc Poems translated into English Chinese, French, Nepali language. Awarded nationally and internationally.

Sengepu Nageswara Rao

Sangepu Nageswara Rao working as Junior Lecturer in English at govt junior college burgampahad it belongs to Badradri kothagudem dist Telangana state.He has been passionate about words ever since he learnt to read Books have fascinated him,and he has been a book worm.He completed M.A ,B.ed from kakatiya university. He qualified TS SET from Telangana state and also AP SET from Andhra Pradesh state.He has writing for several online writing.Married to sunitha and he has two children-Levin Raj and Eliziya Rowan.He compiled two poems.He wrote one novel to web novel.He is always participate social activities from NSS.He is one of the programme officers of NSS.

Shikha Chatterjee

Shikha Chatterjee is Assistant Professor in English in Sam Higginbottom University of Agriculture, Technology and Sciences, Prayagraj, India. She is a trained vocalist in Indian classical music. Her interests include creative writing, painting, singing and travelling. She has collaborated with a renowned scholar of Hindi and Professor in the University of Naples, Italy, for a bilingual book, Bhojpuri Loriki Part-2 currently available in the U.S. Library of Congress.

Sunita Paul

Sunita Paul, author, editor, homemaker, event organiser and publisher from Kolkata, the city of joy Recipient of awards of international repute Sunita is the founder of Aabs Publishing House, Kolkata.

Vandita Dharni

Vandita Dharni obtained her Ph.D. degree from Allahabad Uiversity in American Literature. Several of her articles, poems and short stories have been published in journals like Criterion, Ruminations, GNOSIS, HellBound Publishing House and International magazines like Immagine andPoessia, Synchronised Chaos, Guido Gozzano. and Primer Antologia De Poetas Del Proyecto De Unamos Al Mundo Con La Poesia- Mexico. Her poem, *The Endangered Tiger* was given an honourable mention in the Guido Gozzano. Her first anthology, *Quintessential Outpourings* was published in 2016.Her next two books, *The Oyster of Love*and *Rippling Overtures*have been published recently. Her poems were read on the John Kavanagh show. She has edited anthologies for Poetry World and an anthology entitled *Petals OfPeace*. She has also reviewed several poems on poetry sites like Poetry Review on Facebook. She has been honoured with the Poetic Galaxy Award 2018 by the Literati Cosmos Society for her notable contribution to Poetry and the Double Cross Award for her outstanding contributions in the book on Complexion Based Discriminations. They were conferred upon by the Literati Cosmos Society of India Recently the World Poetic Star award 2019 has also been conferred upon her by the World Nation's Writers' Union.

Vinamrata

She is an Assistant Professor of English in MSKB College, B.R.A. BIHAR University, Bihar, India. Her Ph.D. dissertation is on "Writing Resistance: The Politics of Nation Formation, Racism and Neo-Imperialism in the Fiction of Salman Rushdie" from Banaras Hindu University. She has worked on theories like

Colonialism, Post-colonialism, Imperialism and other such relevant areas. Several research papers have been published under her name. She has developed an insight for Indian English Writers, Mythical Studies as well as Feminist Writings. She has a deep inclination for poetry writing as well as storytelling. Most of her poems deal with questions on Existentialism and Feminist perspective. She started writing poems in Hindi and English from her school days and some of her poems have been published in various anthologies.

Volivoju, Sammaiah Chary
Teacher, Khammam, Telangana

Williamsji Maveli

Williamsji Maveli is the Regional President -Middle East for the global writers platform- Union Hispanomundial De Escritores (UHE) and Founder of WHORLED WIDE WRITERS , world's most active writers forum. He is a member of WORLD NATIONS WRITERS UNION holding an additional honorary member status in their academy World Higher Literary Academic Council (WHLAC). He is currently supporting world wide writers by way of his trilogy named as IN DEPTH, INSIGHT and INSPIRE. He has won many prestigious honorary awards for his literary excellence in literature, both in English as well his Mother-tongue Malayalam. He is currently working as a Freelance web content writer and designer at Bangalore and Cochin in India. Earlier, he had worked for ETISLALAT, THURAYA SATELLITE Corporations, ME PUBLISHERS, KHALEEJ TIMES, GULF NEWS & GULF TODAY – All News Agencies in United Arab Emirates.

Bindi Sharma

Bindi Sharma is M.A. in Political Science. She is a freelance journalist and a bilingual poet, writes in both English and Hindi. She has authored several books. Her poems and articles have been published in various National and International books and journals. She is recipient of many National and International Awards.

Anuradha Banerjee

Anuradha Banerjee, born and brought up in Varanasi obtained her Ph.D in English from Banaras Hindu University. She is former Head of the Department of English, Vasant Kanya Mahavidyalaya, Kamachha, Varanasi. A renowned creative writer, she has composed songs, poems, and written stories, plays, critical articles in Hindi, English, Bengali, Sanskrit and Urdu which are published in many magazines and journals. She has also translated many works in English from various languages and has been felicitated time and again by many prestigious institutions and platforms. She is recipient of many National and International Awards.

Rachna Srivastava

Rachna Srivastava, Principal, Vasant Kanya Mahavidyalaya, obtained her Ph.D from Mahatma Gandhi Kashi Vidyapeeth, Varanasi. She has published four books, edited two books and has published several papers in National and International books and journals. She is an active member of several organisations and NGOs and has been felicitated by various institutions for her valuable contribution in the field of education.

Bina Singh

Dr.Singh Head of the Department of English Vasant Kanya Mahavidyalaya affiliated to BHU Varanasi born and brought up in Varanasi obtained her PhD from BHU. Dr. Singh has authored six books published articles research papers poems in international and national books and journals. Participated, organised and chaired and conducted many international seminars workshops and poetry festivals. Ms. Singh is member of various academic social and cultural bodies. Presently she is the president of Kashi Tatav Sabha, Theosophical Society of India Varanasi.

Purnima Singh

She is an Assistant Professor of English in VasantKanyaMahavidylaya, Kamachha. She has worked on "Consumer Capitalism and Fiction of Ron Rash" as her Ph.D dissertation. A lover of beauty and nature she voices her concern for the conservation of nature in several of her papers published in various reputed International journals and books. She started writing poems in Hindi and English from her college days and won awards for her poems at College and University competitions. Her poems have appeared In *Atunis* and her poem "Unearthly" was published in the volume, *Leaves of thePoet Tree, Season Two*. She recently published a book of verse titled *In Search of Meaning: Poetry by Purnima* with Pen It Publishers. She writes in various genres and several of her short stories have been published with soflayinc. She is also an editor of the website phanishwarnathrenu.com which is a platform for literature enthusiasts to read works of budding author and also share their own work. A member of World Nation Writer's Union, she is dedicated to the cause of spreading love and peace through literature.

Supriya Singh

Supriya Singh is an Assistant Professor in the Department of English, Vasant Kanya Mahavidyalaya, Varanasi. She has received National Government Scholarship and V. Rai memorial scholarship while pursuing her Higher Studies. She is a lover of Humanity and has worked in an American N.G.O. by the name *Magis Sylvestris*, for deaf and dumb students in India. She has worked on 'Gayatri Chakraborty Spivak and the Third World Feminist Discourse'. Her research papers have been published in various national and international journals. She has also served as English lecturer through Uttar Pradesh Public Service Commission. She has actively participated in organizing various national seminars and conferences. She is also an external subject expert of Amity Institute of English Studies and Research, Noida, regarding curriculum design.

Kamala Pandey

Kamala Pandey, former Head of the Department of Sanskrit, Vasant Kanya Mahavidyalaya, Kamachha, Varanasi, obtained her Ph.D from Banaras Hindu University. She is bilingual poet writing in Hindi and Sanskrit and is recipient of many awards and honours given by prestigious institutions. She was honoured by the Government of Uttar Pradesh for her contribution in the field of Sanskrit Literature and Language. Her major works are *Rakshat Gangam, Shrigangadandakam, Bhagwan Shankaracharya Avirbhuyata Punirbhuvi, Dhara Kampate.*

Asha Yadav

Asha Yadav is currently Associate Professor in the Department of Hindi, Vasant Kanya Mahavidyalaya. She obtained her Ph.D from Banaras Hindu University. She is a creative writer and has published many poems, articles and short stories. Her major works are: भारतीय स्त्री:दशा और दिशा ; जीवन बिन्दु(काव्य-संग्रह) ; सर्जना (काव्य-संग्रह) and others. She has received several awards for her scholarship from various prestigious institutions.

Banibrata Mahanta

Banibrata Mahanta teaches English Literature at Banaras Hindu University. His academic interests are in the areas of Nationalism and Visual Culture, Disability Studies and Linguistics and ELT. He has written on disability and old age in literature, the development of Indian nationalist thought, Indian literature in English, and the historical and contemporary developments in English Studies in India. An edited volume, *English Studies in India: Contemporary and Evolving Paradigms*, has been published recently by Springer. An occasional translator, he has translated poems, short stories and novels from Bengali and Hindi into English. He is also written and edited study material for distance learning students on disability and Indian folk literature and culture. He has been part of the Airports Authority of India's English language training for ATCOs at LBS International Airport, Varanasi. He is also involved in developing facilities for disabled students in Banaras Hindu University

Shanta Chatterjee

Shanta Chatterjee is Associate Professor and Head, Department of Sanskrit, VKM. Her poems are published in Sanskrit, Bangla and Hindi.

Nairanjana Srivastava

A student of cultural history of ancient India and a writer by passion. She is Assistant Professor in Vasant Kanya Mahavidyalaya in the Department of AIHC & Archaeology. Recipient of awards like 'Mohan Rakesh Award', 'Mahadevi Verma Samman for Creative Contributions' and 'Kadambini Sahitya Samman' and 'Yuva-Kathakar Puruskar', she has been regularly writing for Akashwani Varanasi and Lucknow Centres.

Pramila Khadun

Pramila Khadun is a poetess from Mauritius. Khadun has published poems in various national and international books. She has authored four collections of poems and one novel titled 'When love speaks'. Currently she has published a book 'Food and Nutrition' for school in Mauritius. She is bilingual poet writes poems in English and French.

Renette Dsouza

Renette Peterson D'Souza - writer and editor, from Mumbai-India. She is also an entrepreneur and social activist for empowerment of women from Mumbai and is a strong believer in the simple policy of 'Live and let live'. With a zest for life and a penchant for writing poetry, she has penned many poems on a broad range of topics on social media and many online worldwide poetry forums and e magazines. Her poems have been read on International platforms like The Dear John Show and have been published in various national as well as international anthologies.

Manju Kumari

Manju Kumari is an Assistant Professor in Sanskrit at Vasant Kanya Mahavidyalaya, Kamachha, Varanasi. She has authored books in Hindi and Sanskrit and also writes poems in Hindi and Sanskrit.